GW00862952

Instagram Marketing 101

Unleash the power of Instagram on your business with more real followers, likes and customers

SAM A. BROWN

CONTENTS

CHAPTER 1
THE ORIGINS OF INSTAGRAM

The name Instagram is a merging of "instant camera" and "telegram" and is based around the principle that pictures can be instantly shared to anyone in the world – just like a telegram can be sent anywhere in the world. The company was founded by Kevin Systrom and Mike Krieger in 2010. Their idea was simply to create a platform for people to share pictures and videos whilst on the move from any location; providing it had internet access. It is possible to add a caption to your picture but in many cases a picture really can say a thousand words. Much like any of the other social media sites Instagram allows people to connect to each other quickly and easily. The difference with Instagram is that the emphasis is on the use of unique, individual pictures to portray your message.

This idea has progressed and grown over the last few years. Whether it was envisioned or not Instagram has made it possible for people to connect on a whole new level. A picture can be so much more primal than words. Words are not always needed when a picture literally takes your breath away. What was originally envisioned as a means of sending photos to each other has now evolved into a place to showcase your talents and connect with other like minded souls – whether for business or personal reasons. The site has retained its simplicity which is part of the appeal to the multitude of users. Anyone with basic computer knowledge can create an account and be uploading pictures in few moments.

Its initial launch in October 2010 was quickly followed in January 2011 with an update and the addition of hashtags. The idea behind this was to enable pictures to have tags added to them relating to their theme. This tag could then be searched upon to locate pictures within a defined subject area. Instagram encourages its users to keep the tags as relevant as possible and not to use generic tags. Several tags can be used in one post but too many tags will make any post look fake and will probably be assumed to be a scam. Variants on these tags have appeared as the site has progressed and it is now possible to track the location of where a picture was taken. Third party software has sprung up to assist in analysing the tags for popularity, relevance and user type. This information can be a valuable assistance to anyone attempting to market a product.

Later that same year Instagram upgraded its software and added in a variety of filters. These filters allow a picture to be instantly edited according to different light settings. Included in this was the option to have the picture in black and white. The filters add a nice touch to any picture often creating a nostalgic or wish you were here type look. By 2012 Instagram was firmly established with approximately thirty million users. Rapid growth has occurred, aided by clever marketing resulting in two million registered users byJanuary2014.This growth continued through 2014and by the end of 2014 this number had swollen to three hundred million. There are currently over a billion photographs on Instagram and all rights are retained by the account holder. Instagram offers its service for free and does not make money from the uploaded photographs. It has pledged to continue offering the service for free for the foreseeable future.

Due to the phenomenal success of Instagram it was acquired by Facebook in 2012. There was an unsuccessful attempt by Facebook to have the rights to uploaded photos and sell them as they saw fit. This decision was quickly reversed due to public protest and the mass of customers closing accounts. Instagram maintains this change of terms was badly worded and they are working to correct this. Facebook spent a large sum of money purchasing Instagram and will, at some point in the future, want to see something back for this investment. Kevin Systrom, the founder of Instagram has remained at the helm even after Facebook purchased it.

Instagram does have competitors in the form of Flickr and Pheed but these do not have the same level of followers and are not as well known. Flickr was bought by Yahoo but has so far failed to deliver in the same way that Instagram has. Instagram is a free app and can be downloaded to any device, although some devices, such as Blackberry 10 and Nokia Symbian devices, may currently need third party software. Part of the success of this formidable platform is its willingness to adapt, innovative and improve.

Instagram, like most internet based software, continues to grow and explore new ways of attracting customers. It has added the ability to send photos directly from one individual to another – a feature which directly competes with Snapchat. It also now allows advertising on the site as a means of generating funds. There are also many options to assist users in involving customers in current activities both to increase the customer base and ensure loyalty.

Weekend Hashtag project is one such attempt. A theme is released to followers every Friday. All users are invited to post pictures which creatively embrace the theme and its associated hashtag. The pictures must be posted by the end of Sunday ready for judging. The best is announced and gets an instant boost in standing and probably in followers too.

Throwback Thursday is another attempt to increase loyalty and the customer base. A user can post any picture of the past as long as it has the hashtag #TBT. The usual pictures are of early childhood or particularly poignant moments or occasions in people's lives. There are a variety of celebrities which have joined in this challenge and ensured its popularity. It allows other users to see some of the events that have happened in your life and shaped you to be the person you are today. The posted pictures do not need to be happy memories; anything is acceptable and will start interaction with other users. This sort of sharing is also very good for establishing the authenticity of Instagrams users. This is a key trait in its rapid growth – people believe in it and the other users.

Selfies has become one of the biggest topics of the year and as even become the word of the year according to the Oxford English Dictionary. A selfie is simply a self portrait and can be done with a phone or a digital camera and uploaded. Again the interest of celebrities in this fun gimmick has done wonders for Instagram's profile. Selfies were originally of the face but they have expanded to be all or any part of the body. This can be a useful tool to show your followers that you are human, blemishes and all. This is essential as clearly being your self is obvious to the other users and this approach gains the trust and credibility you need.

Instagram now also features videos up to fifteen seconds long which can be created and posted by anyone. These videos are usually poignant or funny moments but they are increasingly being used to market a product and the video will demonstrate just how good the product is. More recently video generation tools have been added which allow you to speed up a video – effectively compacting one days filming into 15 seconds. Every picture or video uploaded can be geo-tagged with its longitude and latitude co-ordinates. Every year Instagram will collate this information and release a picture list of the top ten geographical locations where pictures have been taken.

As the marketplace swelled so too did the products available from the company. In 2012 all users were given the ability to make web profiles which effectively allowed Instagram to be a social media site. In 2013 it became possible to link your Instagram account with Facebook, Twitter, Tumblr or Flickr. Also in 2013 was the introduction of Instagram direct.

There was also a new addition in April 2012. The explore tab has up to twenty one photos – which must belong to a public user with a non-private profile. The idea is that Instagram users can search for particular users or hashtags and easily locate others interested in the same fields as you. The 21 photos shown are based on your preferences; the photos you have previously liked and popular trends now. Not everyone sees the same photos, wherever possible Instagram shows you products which are linked to you profile and this ensures everyone sees a slightly different finished product.

There is a huge range of features available but filters seem to have dominated the market as of late. There are hundreds of different filters ranging from natural light to Earlybird, a filter which improves pink coverage and provides pictures an older look with a warm feel.

CHAPTER 2
THE POWER INSTAGRAM HAS ON YOUR BUSINESS

Instagram does not provide you with a direct marketing possibility. It is not possible to provide links to your own website or to publish content pushing consumers towards your products. The site is all about the power of the photo. Whilst at first this may seem like it has no affect on your business it actually has a lot of potential. Social media is essential for any business, without it there are huge sections of the market which will simply not know you exist. A modern business needs to have an online presence. Without this they may miss out on the younger generation of shoppers and lose the opportunity to utilise social media as a giant marketing machine. The following five items will assist you in harnessing the power of Instagram and promoting your business to the widest possible audience.

Photos

Instagram is a photo based site. This means that all the usual advertising methods will not work. You will not be able to create a clever sales picture which will suck customers in and persuade them to purchase. The picture must do all the work for you. This is both the greatest strength and weakness of the site. Your advertising staff must stretch their imaginations to come up with ways of promoting your product through picture. The more beautiful or soul searching the picture the more likely that followers will like it and consider purchasing your product. Starbucks are an excellent example of a company getting it right. The picture of a coffee with cake presented immaculately triggers a need inside of people. This combines with a simple caption that mentions Starbucks and asks other users to upload their own coffee photos with a tag. This results in driving Starbucks products into the hearts and minds of consumers. If you can achieve this then you have captured your audience and just need to lead them to your product.

It is always a good idea to utilise the filters available in Instagram. They can change the perspective of a picture and how it is seen by other users. More importantly the filters on Instagram are fairly unique and people will automatically know it is an Instagram picture and respond accordingly.

Hashtags

When uploading pictures there is no option in Instagram to create a link which can make it far harder to market around the company. It is not possible to hyperlink a URL in a description or comment. The URL can appear but you will not be able to click on it and go to the web page. The only link permissible is the one included in your initial set up of your account and this should be to your main website. This link will always appear next to your name and your name should be chosen carefully. It cannot be changed! Instagram places all the emphasis on hashtags and the pressure on businesses to get the hashtag market right. Instagram photos can together make up a marketing campaign. Each photo must have a hashtag which associates it with the other photos and associates it with the product you are attempting to promote. The idea of this marketing campaign is for your picture to inspire followers to upload their own pictures and subconsciously create links between the pictures and your products. This subconscious link will ensure you gain actual sales. In this aspect it is essential to have as many pictures as possible associated with your brand. For this you will need as many followers as possible and a good enough marketing picture that many others will be persuaded to join you. The emphasis here is on a truly stunning picture.

Key words in your caption must have hashtags on either side of them to allow the search functions to work properly. It is not advisable to have too many hashtags as this will may your post look like spam. It will also make it hard to read your caption and will detract from the message you are sending out. Research suggests that between four and ten hashtags are a good number. Instagram will also link with other major social sites like Facebook and Twitter to enable your hashtags to connect to searches in these alternative social media sites. Even if you do not have an account on these sites you can still become known on them.

It is possible to aggregate photos on your own website and then to create a mirage of many pictures. Properly combined it will make a stunning backdrop which will draw people to your product. There are also products on Instagram which can be found via the search function which allow you to find and repost hashtagged content. This can ensure your images, linked via similar hashtags remain at the top of the search pages.

Purchasing power

Once you have established a brand hashtag you may find some followers submit photos with your branded hashtag displayed. This keeps the relationship fresh and it is important to respond to these users as this builds loyalty as well as recognition. As with most social platforms the more followers you gain the higher you will appear in listings and searches. Ensuring this level of contact with your customers and followers will plant subconscious seeds which will bear fruit when the user is looking at which product to purchase.

Of course, there is more to selling your product than just keeping the product fresh in potential customer's minds. Collecting followers and Instagram postings may keep you very busy but for it to be truly effective you need sales. One of the best ways of doing this is to utilise a triggered response. The triggered response will monitor the user content and place a message on the photo aimed at specific users to encourage them to either participate or purchase your product. Alternatively it is possible to use third party software to monitor profile tags and hashtags. This will enable you to respond manually to the relevant users. The important thing to remember here is that a message should be genuine and offer a reward for their participation or purchase. Potential customers may not need your product at that moment in time but a good offer will ensure they purchase it anyway.

Content

Instagram is an online platform for real people. People who may not know each other in the physical world can connect and communicate on Instagram. People respond to other user's suggestions particularly if they have a large following. The same process must be utilised by your business. There is limited potential in posting pictures of celebrities linked to your product. In the majority of cases people will not be able to relate to them. However if you post a picture from one of your followers you have genuine content and genuine comments. Your sales will grow simply because online users can relate to the product and see themselves wearing or using it. A hashtag will ensure people find the product and they can be directed to a purchase point. A picture which is awe inspiring or particularly beautiful will receive the best response. It must be a genuine picture that will stop people in their tracks but that they can relate to.

Connecting with Instagram

Instagram may not offer the opportunity to directly market your products. It does provide a site where genuine people can connect with each other. This authenticity is the reason the site is so popular. The simplest way to add this into your marketing structure is to request your followers submit photos and videos of themselves in your products. Non-followers are welcome to do so too! This will generate increased interest on Instagram but will also provide opportunity for people to go to your own site to survey the products on offer. The selling point is on your own site where visitors can find Instagram users displaying their use of the product. Your site instantly becomes more genuine and inviting. With no real effort a new customer will perceive you as authentic and reliable, simply because other Instagram users have the same feeling. This environment of trust will result in sales. Of course having a high profile presence on a social media site will mean you need to continually respond and interact with these customers. In particular negative comments should be dealt with promptly and fairly to ensure it does not damage your blossoming reputation.

Social media has become a significant presence in everyday lives. There are many people who check their preferred social media sites the moment they wake up and cannot go half an hour without checking what is going on. In fact the majority of your potential customers will check a social media site at least once a day. There is no other product on the planet which has the potential to influence so many people simultaneously and so regularly.

Whilst maintaining a profile on Instagram will be time consuming it would be ridiculous not to attempt to reach the potential customers available. If your account is handled correctly then, other than the time cost, this is a free marketing opportunity. It has the power to keep your business name in front of many people daily and will allow your business to be more than a business. It will become a personality to your followers. They will tweet and re-tweet pictures relevant to your business. This inadvertently promotes your business and works because they are not doing it for that reason. To the Instagram user it is simply an opportunity to interact with another user and be entertained and informed.

It is also true that the brain can read a picture many times faster than it can assimilate the written word. A picture will literally say a thousand words and need only be in front of someone for a few seconds. These few seconds can be the start of a new relationship, how many businesses can afford to miss this potential.

Another important factor to consider is that the internet and all of its glorious content is now available to people at any time of day from practical anywhere in the world. A local advertising campaign will affect your local area. A television campaign may affect a whole country but a social media campaign can be seen by the whole world. It has always been true that the more sales pitches you make the more sales you will have, even if your conversion rate is only 1%. A social media site offering you the world is about as big a platform and potential customer base as you can currently get!

The availability of the internet also allows you to make a post at any time of the day or night. Whenever something appears in front of you which you believe will make a good picture you can snap it on your phone and upload it. This allows both for impromptu marketing opportunities and keeps your online presence maintained, building the personality of your business. Ultimately you may never be disconnected from your customers but you will provoke a loyalty in them as they feel they know you and your business.

The ultimate power of Instagram for your business is that you don't know who will come across your posting. Time spent building marketing campaigns, followers and making posts are all excellent ways to market your products. However, occasionally the picture you upload in the morning may have just the right hashtag to bring it to the attention of someone who has not previously heard of you. This someone may have the power to change your business for the better whether through financial backing or an endorsement or even a complimentary product. Instagram enables you to reach out and leaves you open to any and all prospects. You will simply have to decide if they are of interest to you or not.

Possibly the most important piece of advice when building an Instagram business profile is to ensure you have high quality content. Pictures and captions need to be considered carefully to ensure they portray the right message and will not invoke too controversial a response. Debate is a useful tool for keeping your pictures and business in the limelight. Too much controversy may work against the genuine image you are trying to build. You should also remember to comment on other user's pictures whether there products and postings compliment yours or not. This will ensure you build a good reputation and not just be seen as a marketing force. If you are leaving favourable comments with unconnected users it is likely that they will at least look at your postings and you may gain a new fan or many fans if they host a popular account.

CHAPTER 3
HOW TO GET MORE ORGANIC FOLLOWERS

It is fairly obvious that for any social media marketing campaign to even stand a chance of working you will need followers. Without these your best marketing efforts will be falling on deaf ears. There are several methods which will assist you in obtaining followers:

Like other photos

The first port of call is the popular photos and posts. The more popular the photo the more followers they will probably have. By liking the photo you will have let others know of your presence. There is a good chance that some of these followers will look at your profile and may start to follow you. It is important to respond to any comments to ensure you start building a rapport with your new followers.

It is also a good idea to use the explore function and look for themes and pictures you actually like. Again you will need to like these and hope that some will become your followers. It should be easy to make comments and witty remarks in this section as you are familiar with the topic and presumably have some knowledge or opinion you can pass on.

A third option is to search by tags. This will allow you to click through a list and like many pictures very quickly and may result in many followers. Of course, it will be much harder to interact with these followers if you build this list quickly and that may mean some dropping off later on.

You will need to repeat this procedure daily in order to build a good level of followers.

Comment on photos

Whilst liking will encourage people to look at your profile and possible follow you talking to them will have far more long lasting results. It will not be possible to comment on thousands of photos daily but you can comment on the ones you particularly like or are in your field of expertise.

It is important to make nice, flattering comments and nothing negative. You are attempting to build a rapport with other users! It is best to stay away from the generic 'nice pic' type comment and instead focus on making a comment actually relevant to the picture. The receiver of this comment is bound to be flattered and will want to reply, possibly look at your profile and maybe even follow you! You will need to follow up on this and reply to their reply. This is guaranteed to build a rapport, which will ensure they follow you and inform their friends and followers of their latest discovery.

Captions

It is vital to add captions to your own pictures. Just as you are responding to others they will respond to you. There are countless other users out there looking to build their fan base and there is no reason why this cannot be mutually beneficial. **Comments should be kept short or the reader will lose interest.** A location might ensure the picture can be placed in context. A shot explanation of the inspiration will probably receive some responses. The most effective way of obtaining responses is to ask a question. Ask if others have used a particular place or product or whether someone has an opinion on which shoes should be worn today. Anything that is posed as a question will provoke a response. It is important not to pose questions on anything too political or sensitive at this stage – you want to build friends not sparring partners. Finally a caption should include a call to action if possible. If you have posted a picture of your bad parking invite others to post their pictures. If doing this you will need to make sure that others will use your tag by saying something along the lines of "show me your bad parking – use the tag #carsontop".

Postings

You will obviously never gain followers or retain the ones you have if you never post anything. A follower needs to feel part of your life and have something to read and comment on. If not there are plenty of other posts they can follow. However, just as you need to post you can post too often. You should never post more than one picture at a time and set a maximum of ten photos per day. One photo is enough to keep interest and too many will clog up your followers news feeds. This will quickly wind them up and ensure they stop following you. It is also essential that all photos are special and unique. This ensures a response and growth of followers. Posting too many either means they are not unique or that they are unbelievable.

Timing

A fantastic picture can occur anytime. It may be the most amazing sunset you have ever seen but you will need to think about whether it is the best time to post your picture. To gather responses from your followers and to gain new ones you need to be posting when the majority of people are online. There are tools available on line to find out the peak usage time of your followers although this is of limited use when you are trying to build followers. Most people will be online before and after work, quite possibly during the commute to and from work. Most pictures will be buried in a users news feed within three or four hours of being posted and if not viewed by then will probably not be. Time your postings accordingly.

Shoutouts

On Instagram it is possible for you to 'shoutout' about another person's account. In effect you are telling your followers about this account and that they should follow it. The ideal behind this is that if you do it for someone then they will return the favour. There is no guarantee so pick the account carefully! Although it would be extremely beneficial to shoutout for a celebrity it is unlikely you will receive the return favour. Instead pick accounts that will compliment your offering and have similar interest, but not identical. You can even comment on a few of their pictures and then ask them for a shoutout by saying "follow me and I'll follow back".

Themes

Your account will need a theme, most likely your business products and the pictures you post should all remain on that theme. This is important to your followers as they begin to follow you for what is on your profile. They will keep coming back as they know what to expect. If you are inconsistent they will quickly stop following you and look elsewhere as they do not want their time wasted looking at irrelevant material on your account. A constant theme is their guarantee that they will actually be interested in what you are posting. If your business would benefit from several themes that will simply not work together it is possible to have more than one Instagram account although this will require building followers for both accounts as they may not subscribe to both themes.

The Bio

When you first create your account you will need to choose an appropriate username and set the link to your business site. There is also the option to set a bio. This is important as it will tell others what it is you are interested and what they can expect from your site. This will assist in their decision whether to follow you or not so ensure the content is accurate and specific.

Friends

An obvious place to start building followers is whether you have any friends, business colleagues, suppliers or customers with accounts. It should be easy to follow them and ask them to follow you back. This will create instant followers and the potential to gain some of their followers. Facebook or Twitter can also be a good source of friends which should follow you.

There are also suggestions made by Instagram as to which accounts you might like to follow. If you are genuinely interested in these accounts then follow them and hope they return the favour. It is important not to go overboard with regards to following people. You need more followers than you are following or you may clog your news feed and miss the important posts.

Social networks

Instagram already provides a link with Facebook and Twitter via the hashtags but if you have other social media profiles it is advisable to link them all together. Once they are all synched you any picture you post to Instagram will automatically appear on the other social media sites. This creates a far bigger audience and potential for followers with no extra effort.

Tags

As previously mentioned tags are an essential part of the power of Instagram. Using tags will allow other users to find your account and potentially follow you. Tags need to be relevant to the picture and your theme to ensure you attract the sort of person who wants to follow you. It can also be very useful to check which tags are popular at the moment and if at all possible use them in your postings. This will automatically piggy back your post onto other posts with large followings and may create additional followers. As you are attempting to build a solid account with a good reputation it is advisable to avoid using tags, no matter how popular, which have no relevance to your pictures.

There are apps that will provide you with a list of the most popular tags of the day and the second most popular. These can be useful to ensure you mention some of these tags in your postings that will gain interest in your posts. Again, these tags should only be used if they are relevant to your pictures.

It may be of use to note that it is possible to go back to an old picture and add a tag to it, which will make it relevant again. This is worth considering if a trending tag for the day can be used in an old picture but not your fresh post.

Tagging

A variation of the tags is to create your own tag. This needs to be relevant to your theme and business. If you are selling cake stands then a hashtag such as #cakestandsrule may be appropriate. If you add this hashtag to every one of your postings you will quickly have created your own hashtag. The hope would then be that others adopt your hashtag on their own similar pictures and your account is opened to many new, like minded followers.

Pictures

It has already been mentioned that pictures need to be unique and amazing but there are a few tips to improve your pictures. The better the picture the more likely you will gain additional followers. Human beings love symmetry and wherever possible you should attempt to include this in your pictures. A photo should always be simple. Too many items in a photo will distract from the one you want your followers to look at. Equally a different perspective of something will add mystery to your photo. Just make sure that the focus of the picture is still visible. It is also advisable to download some software for merging photos. Then you will be able to share complimentary products in one picture and increase your likelihood of comments and followers

Filters are also important. This is not just to advertise to potential followers that this is an Instagram photo. If you choose just two or three filters and use them every time then your followers and potential followers will appreciate the uniformity of your account. As with the theme, people will know what they are getting and be happy to return to your post.

Building followers is all about getting your pictures in front of as many people as possible but it must always be done with your business image and reputation in mind. A genuine post will receive much more long term attention than any post perceived to be artificial. The same values you run your business by need to be applied to your Instagram account.

CHAPTER 4
WHICH POSTS GAIN THE MOST ATTENTION?

In the four years since its inception Instagram has gained millions of followers and billions of pictures. The first post to get more than one million likes was from celebrity bad boy Justin Bieber in 2013 and was of him posing with the legendary actor Will Smith. Since then he has got over one million likes on several posts. Obviously his account has a huge head start in terms of followers and notoriety. The average person or business will simply not be able to create that draw at the start. This does not mean that the posts which gain the most attention are just from celebrities. There are over, very popular posts with huge followings. The issue is how do you make your posts one of these? The answer to this is in understanding what makes these posts gain so much attention:

Popularity

You don't need to be Justin Bieber or J-Lo to get the best posts. You need followers. The more followers you have the more that will potentially like your post. The more likes you have the more you increase your chances of having one of the posts which attracts the most attention. It is also possible to tap into the followers of your followers to boost your popularity.

Topical

A great way of having the next best post is to be one of the first on a new topic. You will need a current, relevant topic which will interest many Instagram users not just your followers. This works even better if you create a hashtag which others use in similar posts. This will act as a link introducing more users to your post. The only way to achieve this is to be monitoring the web and jump o any opportunity which has the potential to provoke the required response. It is not enough to be following the daily most popular and trying to tie into the keywords. You need to be creating the most popular.

Seasonal

Hits on social media sites increase dramatically at seasonal holiday times. Christmas, Thanksgiving and many other festivals throughout the year all provide additional opportunities to post material. The holiday periods also provide more time for people to look at posts and like or comment. Having a post that relates to a seasonal holiday will increase the number of hits and potential likes and followers.

Tags

Hashtags are an extremely important part of Instagram. To ensure you post is one of the top attention gatherers you will need to put several highly relevant hashtags in your caption. Ideally these tags will all be on the top tags for the day which will attract more users and potential likes. In principle the more hashtags you use the more your pictures will be viewed. Of course viewing is not the same as liking and your post will never gain popularity if it is never liked. Equally your picture will be lost in a sea of pictures if you use the wrong hashtag and careful thought should be given to this element.

The right photo

You will never manage to have a top rating post if you post pictures that people do not want to look at. There are several third party software apps which will assist in providing information on the most popular picture. A simple rule of thumb is to always put your best picture on the site and never multiple pictures of the same thing. Pictures of the highest quality tend to get the most likes. Equally pictures showing cute pets, family members, unique views or particularly appeal products get the most views. Combined pictures also receive a lot of attention as they tell a story and provide authenticity.

Buy your way to the most popular

It is possible to buy likes via third parties. For a relatively small fee you can purchase 1000 likes and boost the visibility of your photo. This may assist in getting your photo noticed and allowing others to like it but it will never replace organic likes and never create a top post. It can only be a foundation or starting block in the process.

Previous most popular

As with many things it is possible to look back and see which photos or types of postings have gained the most attention over the last four years. Fitting your picture into one of these trends will certainly help your chances of becoming the most popular.

Selfies – This trend was effectively started by Ellen Degeneres with some big Hollywood actors at the Oscars. Since then there have been many selfies, individual and groups. Kim Kardashian took this a step further with a selfie focusing on her bottom. To have an incredibly popular post simply thing of a new angle on this favourite.

Wedding photos always get favourable responses. Romantic happy pictures tug the bow strings of any heart and will get the likes flowing. Even wedding announcements can get excellent responses especially if this is the vessel for telling all and sundry.

Science and the solar system – This is very much about the uniqueness of the photos and the information provided as to what can be seen in the solar system and beyond. The pictures may be amazing but this topic also touches on that big question of "Are we alone?"

Triumphant pictures are always well received. This is particularly true if that triumph is the common person over the state or a large corporation. The underdog story will always be a powerful motivator.

Slightly controversial pictures are excellent for gaining popularity. The picture that poses a question of morality will always gain a large following as everyone will want their say. This is an area to be careful of though. If you pick too delicate a subject it can lead to a bad response and will not assist in building your reputation on Instagram.

Romance pictures, just like weddings are always in demand. In a world of increasing pressures on time and resources a little romance can go a long way. Pictures in this vein allow people to stop and remind themselves of what is really important.

Pets are generally cute. Anything they do which is cute can be photographed and put on Instagram. The response will be a huge number of hits along with plenty of ooohs and aaahs. This acts as another tug on the heartstrings.

The final trend is for happy pictures. Whatever makes a smile and show happiness will make for a good Instagram picture. If it makes you smile it will probably make others smile and like your picture. From then on it will be a snowball effect. Happiness and smiling are contagious and this is why they make such excellent Instagram offerings.

CHAPTER 5
INSTAGRAM MARKETING TOOLS AND TECHNIQUES

Having established your account and started to work on building your following you may well now be looking for additional tips and marketing tools which will assist in building your online presence and your business. You are not alone, Instagram has recognised that many businesses are realising the power of Instagram and are entering the world of social media in an attempt to capitalise on the opportunities available. Instagram have now produced their own blog to provide tips, brand spotlights and news. This is a valuable source of information and should be looked at regularly. The following tools and techniques will also be of benefit:

Balance

Business is a serious affair but if every picture you post is serious your following will be limited to only those seriously interested in your products. Every business needs to learn to balance the fun with the serious side. Fun pictures will generate more hits and serious pictures can have an element of fun. The balance between the two is important to ensure you are followed and taken seriously. It is even possible to utilise one of the most popular trends to balance these two elements. For example if you sell hats post a picture of someone holding a cute puppy and wearing one of your hats. You will receive comments on both.

It is important to use software to track the level of engagement on your postings and pictures. This will provide you with valuable information regarding what obtains responses and sales and what doesn't.

Video

The ability to post short, fifteen minute videos to Instagram is relatively new but an excellent tool in a business arsenal. Videos can provide more insight into a set of events. They can be used to push a promotional opening or discount day and to very quickly show a variety of products. Again the balance between fun and business must be present. The video needs to be of high quality and easily related to. These videos can also be embedded into your own website to create a link between your site and your Instagram account. Not only might this attract more followers it will ensure your marketing video is on show to as many people as possible.

External Apps

As with most things in the digital world there are now apps to allow you and your followers to exploit the most out of the social media world. There are apps which will allow you to search for pictures based on hashtags and keywords. You can then be taken directly to the Instagram account. This would be a useful addition to a website directing people's searches to Instagram. Other apps allow the user to receive instant notifications when new postings are submitted. This ensures people are connecting in real time and don't miss an important announcement. The list is endless and will continue to grow but a little time and research will reveal an app that has a use to you and your business.

Participation

An excellent way to improve followers and raise the profile of your business is to encourage customer participation. The questions and hashtags you enter with your captions should encourage your customers to respond. Customers can be encouraged to make improvement suggestions and exchange information. Creating a two way dialect with your customers will increase rapport and make it far more likely they will spend money with you. The obvious additional benefit is that one happily interacted customer will lead to many more.

Awareness

Being on Instagram is already a marketing tool. Just posting regularly and generating followers will result in your business being mentioned and talked about more than it would have been otherwise. Publicity like this is very difficult to buy and is a gold mine when it comes to generating customers. An additional way to improve you following and keep your name in their minds is to create contests. Using hashtags and pictures it is very easy to create a contest for the best picture on a certain theme. The winner can receive a discount voucher for your products.

Promotion

Instagram is not just good for building an online presence. It can be utilised to promote a physical show or exhibition. Just one posting mentioning it will create a wave of interest. Add to this by promising a discount on entry or on purchases on the day providing the hashtag is mentioned and your exhibition is guaranteed to be a success. It will certainly help your online following as well.

Staff and friends

Just one cute picture which hits the right note can turn a failing business around with the amount of free publicity generated. A free way to market the business is to ask your employees and friends to post pictures either on the company account or their own accounts. These pictures will need hashtags linking them to the business account and potentially the website. You will not only increase your online profile you will portray a human side to the business and encourage you employees to be more involved in the business.

Launch products

Instagram can be an exceptionally good tool for assisting with a launch of a new product or an open day. Make it exclusive and release a short video of you getting the product ready pre release leading up to the actual release of the new product. This can be in one short video or several videos showing the days building up to the release. It won't matter where your customers are in the world they will feel part of something special and it is guaranteed to attract some new customers.

Partnerships

It is important to link up with other business offering complimentary products or even the same product if feasible. Complimentary products will enable sales promotions based on if customers purchase both items and a wider audience as you both utilise each other's followers. Linking with someone who offers the same product as you need not be bad for business. A visible connection can help with promoting an image of trustworthiness. It can also be used as a basis for pictures; a friendly rivalry is bound to attract interest from Instagram users and may even result in picking up some tips.

Pose questions

Instead of coming across as the authority on a certain subject ask your followers questions. The questions can range from "have you used this product today?" to "which product is better". Provoking a response is an excellent marketing tool. People love to be involved and feel that they have something valuable to say. Encouraging this will improve your reputation and following. All of which will definitely not harm your sales.

Alternative posts

Rather than the standard post it can sometimes be useful to mix it up a little. Posting a picture asking people to suggest a caption or to fill in the missing words in a caption will capture people's attention. Users who were not previously followers will join in and follow you, particularly if you are offering a prize. Competitions have always been used as part of marketing strategy this simply places a digital spin onto it.

Geotagging

An excellent marketing strategy is to geotag all pictures and identify where your customers live. You will then be able to use this information to target them with more specific products based on seasonality or research of a given area. Customers will be impressed and more likely to spend with you if they believe you are attempting to get to know them and their needs.

Target offline shoppers

If you have a physical presence on the high street it is possible that some of these shoppers do not connect with you on Instagram. By placing QR codes in store they will be directed towards your website and social media accounts. The rewards for them are discounts which they would not otherwise get. This should translate into them both converting their friends to your products and the additional followers will assist you with your Instagram marketing campaigns.

Make your followers famous

It is possible to run a different competition every month. The winner of this competition will obtain a prize but with their consent you could also put them on your website and announce to the world that they are a winner and how they won the prize. It is also a nice touch to include a section of their bio from their Instagram page. Their fame may only last the month but there are few people who would not enjoy the notoriety and plenty who will follow you just for the chance.

Do not be discouraged if you are currently using offline marketing strategies. Many of the techniques used in the physical world can be utilised online. One of the most important aspects to remember is to be fresh and original. Whether it is a picture, a contest or some other marketing outreach always try to approach it with an angle that hasn't been tried before. Social media users have seen a lot of the same old thing and many will follow a new idea simply because it is fresh. There are marketing companies who will assist in creating and managing your Instagram account and their services can be invaluable to the novice. They will know many tips and shortcuts which will help build your social presence and a large following. Should you wish to utilise one of the services it is advisable to ensure you retain the rights to your account and can easily take back control of it. As your understanding of this marketing tool grows you may wish to pursue your own direction and will need to regain control.

Of equal importance is to remember that although you are just entering information into a computer you are still dealing with real people. People love to be engaged and involved. Never just tell them facts, always come across as their friend and confidant. You need to be someone who can offer them advice and will take their advice back. Recognising them as a person and receiving the recognition back is the strongest marketing tool available. Price will not matter if a customer believes you are genuine and have their best interests at heart.

Instagram has millions of users and it may take time and perseverance to build a good reputation and decent following. There will doubtless be mistakes made upon the way but these mistakes can be used to improve your future campaigns. When things go wrong add the pictures to your account and ask your followers for help. Not only will you obtain free advice but you will confirm your human side. You will show them you are vulnerable and open to advice. This will provide a great foundation for future campaigns as these followers will feel valued and assist in rebuilding your reputation or following. Building a solid foundation of between two and five thousand followers will be the toughest part but properly done will bring many benefits to your business.

CHAPTER 6
REACHING OUT TO POPULAR INSTAGRAM ACCOUNTS

Of course the ultimate aim of your Instagram account is to reach as many people as possible and create as many sales opportunities as possible. As fun as the photos and social interaction is you are in business to make money. There are several Instagrammers who have become very well established and are both respected an influential. The long term plan should be to become one of these. The short term plan involves reaching out to these and tapping into their followers. The association should gain credibility for your business.

Business which have this kind of standing do not need to say yes to everyone wanting to link to them. They will be likely to have over 100,000 followers and this along confirms they offer a quality product or service and have mastered sharing it with the Instagram world. They can afford to be choosy about who they link with as they have many people chasing them. Instagrammers who have gained reputations like this are now being chased by advertisers looking for a way into the Instagram market place. There is no doubt an association with them will be of benefit to your account but how do you go about connecting to them?

The first step is to identify the right Instagrammer to target. There are numerous third party software apps available to assess which accounts have the biggest following. There are also apps which search on hashtags. Combining both these searches will enable you to target accounts which have similar interests to your own. This will make it far easier to connect with them.

It should be noted that many of the highest profile Instagrammers are celebrities or very big named brands. It is possible although difficult to create associations with the big brands. It is a lot harder to get a celebrity to follow you. They are used to being followed and usually do not do the following.

Reaching out

One way of reaching out to a popular account is to look at what you have that they might want or better, need. You will be unable to offer them additional followers unless you have already built up a large following but you may have something else that they need. If they are interested in what you are offering then you will be able to barter and ask for something in return. Your main aim is an association so that some of their massive following will start to follow you. This approach will require some research into what they do and what they like so that you can make an offer which will genuinely interest them. It might be that you will need to pay them to provide some pictures for you or to run your account for a set period of time. This can be a good tactic provided the end result is more followers for you.

Depending upon the product you are selling it may be possible to reach out to these influential Instagrammers and ask them to guest post on your account. Their followers will instantly be looking at your account and possibly follow you. When picking a popular account to try this with you will need to think carefully about the audience attracted to their account and whether any of that audience are likely to be interested in your product. You do not need to pay someone to guest post on your account. If your product or service is close to their heart then they may wish to do it for free. It may be enough for them to know that they are helping to make the world a better place.

Alternatively, if your product is something that they might appreciate then you could provide them with a free sample in exchange for the guest post. Or they may be interested in a supply of your product for the next x amount of months and in return will include pictures on their blog of the product and use your hashtag.

You should also now your own followers. It is possible that one of your followers is actually an influential Instagrammer or that one of yours is connected to a highly followed account. Checking this will not only mean you are already linked and should be able to tap into this potential it will also ensure that you are looking after your own followers. There is no point trying to attract thousands more followers if you are not satisfying the ones you already have.

Shoutouts have been previously mentioned as a tool to try and build followers. This is also an exceptionally good way of reaching out to the most influential Instagram posts and simply asking them to help you. Again you will need to pick your target account based on it having similar likes to your own account. Most influential Instagrammers are still normal people who are happy to help others with their own projects.

Even the biggest accounts on Instagram would like more followers. Many of these accounts are run by individuals with a passion for something. They may have limited exposure outside of Instagram and this can be used to good effect. Assuming you have a website you could offer to post some of their pictures with appropriate captions on your website. You effectively make them famous, albeit briefly. This will raise their profile outside of Instagram and when they mention it to their fans it will have a positive effect on your own following.

When you utilise the popularity app in Instagram you will be able to locate the popular accounts which have relevance to your own business. Having located the accounts you need to check the bio for these accounts and you may find contact information. Contact information usually means they are open to advertising products and forming partnerships. Never broach this subject on Instagram. The email address given should be the best way to contact them. Obviously not all influential accounts choose to feature products so the approach should be made tactfully. If you hit them like a bull in a china shop you risk some bad publicity on their next post. An email should simply state that you are a fan of theirs and that you have recently started up an online store. The second paragraph should mention how much you love one of your own products and whether they would be happy to have a free sample. In return, if they like it as much as you do you should be grateful if they would let their followers know.

Although celebrities are less likely to follow you it does not mean that they will not. Unless you are lucky enough to be selling something they would want then your posts will have to either appeal to their sense of humour or their morality. A carefully worded plea on behalf of what you stand for can produce surprising results. You should never create a request for association based on your own needs. Always place the emphasis on those less fortunate.

Finally you can reach out to any account, influential or not by creating a hype that they would wish to join in. Be straightforward and upfront about what you want. For example if one of the most influential accounts is for ladies shoes and you are a man then start a campaign. It should state if you get x amount of followers before a certain date you will walk a mile in one of these pairs of shoes. A fifteen second video will be posted onto your account and the influential account. People will connect with this real life gesture and even the most influential account holder will see the benefit of being associated with a campaign guaranteed to get a high response.

The one account which is often missed is Instagrams own account. It is actually the most popular account on Instagram and is happy to share images from other users to raise profiles. Simply approach this account with your story. The motivation behind your business or the creation of your business and let them do the rest. This guarantees exposure to the majority of Instagram users and could result in an explosion of personal followers.

CHAPTER 7
CONVERTING FOLLOWERS TO CUSTOMERS

The focus so far has been on how to build a large following. The assumption is that a large following will equate to increased sales. However, this is not always the case. People do not generally go on Instagram to purchase items; they are usually interested in the latest news and gossip displayed via pictures. Large followings do generally indicate a trustworthy and respected presence but this is of scant comfort to the business owner investing many man hours into an Instagram profile.

There is no direct selling possible on Instagram but there are several tried and tested methods and strategies for converting your followers into customers:

Exclusivity

Make it known that Instagram is the place you will launch new products or re-launch old ones and stick to this. Your followers at Instagram will be inspired to know that they saw it first and they will be able to inform others of your latest developments. This approach will build brand loyalty and will inspire followers to look further at your products and potentially become customers. If it is at all possible you should launch a new product live on Instagram – upload several photos or a short video of the launch and then provide Instagram users with a discount code. You will need to tell them that this code is only available via Instagram.

A step above the rest

People want to connect to other people who they believe are genuine. They also want to connect to those who appear to be awesome. A follower will quickly be turned into a customer if he believes your business is a step above the rest. It is a fun filled place to work and somewhere they would like to work. This can be shown by regularly uploading pictures of the staff doing normal activities but having fun whilst doing it. This can be work activities or out of work activities – both have a powerful effect.

A slight spin off from the above tactic is to offer a sneak peak at your latest development or some of your research meetings. Short videos can show the staff involved in these projects. A few pictures can show the product development and inspire many followers to convert to customers. It is even possible to compile a short video demonstration to really connect with your followers.

Involve your followers. Make them want your product by offering it as a prize for the person who makes the best suggestion for an alternative use for the product. Not only will those who didn't win want to buy one but many others may be interested in becoming customers to use it with one of the alternative purposes in mind.

It is also possible to turn followers into customers via the competitions previously mentioned. If you encourage users to post picture on a given theme with your product in their hand then many will enter in order to win the prize. Of course to be in with a chance of getting the price they will need to purchase one of your products to include in the picture. The follower is converted to a customer before they have even realised.

A tactic which invariably works is all about raising the bar. Everyone loves the idea of going to a red carpet movie premier or a photo shoot and being the centre of attention. Maybe you have always dreamed of visiting a very upmarket hotel and have not yet been able to do so. If you make your pictures reminiscent of these settings people will automatically wish they were at the spectacular event in the picture and will buy products just to keep that feeling of being there.

It is also imperative you check what your fans are posting. It is highly likely that some of them have already posted pictures of themselves with your product. Use these pictures and their captions on your own feed to assist in creating that feeling of authenticity and credibility. These pictures can also be added to your own website which will encourage others to take pictures of themselves with your product in the hope of being on your site. This is an appeal to the vanity of your followers and usually has very positive results.

An often overlooked way to turn followers into customers is to encourage them to reach out to you. Questions and even advice should be welcomed from your followers. Wherever possible concerns should be addressed in your posts and if decent suggestions are made implement them. Whether the suggestion is a change of colour on the sole of a shoe or for the company to host a music festival it is important to respond and if viable to actually follow through on the suggestion. Giving your consumers the power to feel involved in your business will turn them into customers via loyalty and respect.

Whilst exclusivity is a powerful tool it is important to connect to other social media sites as well. There are many users on Facebook who are not yet on Instagram. To ensure you capitalise on every opportunity to turn a follower into a customer you should be posting something on all sites, even if that something is directing everyone to Instagram for the exclusive offers. This will tap into the people who do not have Instagram accounts but now need one as they want your product. On creating an account they will boost your following figures as well as convert from follower to customer.

Most importantly you need to know your fan base and ensure all those listed as following do actually check your postings. The follower who has purchased something but has since not looked at one of your posts is ripe for conversion. They liked your product enough to purchase it but have not felt engaged enough to continue following you. They may still be listed as a follower but analysis will show they no longer purchase anything. These sorts of potential customers can be reached by looking at what they purchased and when. You will then be able to create another similar situation with an exclusive discount and convert your follower back into a customer.

CHAPTER 8
THE FUTURE OF INSTAGRAM

In just four years Instagram has gone from nothing to being arguably the most important social media site for businesses. The success of it originates from its simplicity and the fact that anyone can use it and can control whether a picture is reused elsewhere or not. There is no doubt that the celebrity additions to Instagram have helped in its success.

Signing up is free and will remain so but adverts are now appearing on the site as a way for Facebook (the owners of Instagram) to start earning money. There have already been rumours of a 'buy' button on Facebook which will allow users to purchase items with one click and without leaving the page they were on. Is this an option for Instagram in the future?

Instagram, guided by its parent company Facebook, will continue to grow and develop. The online market place shows no sign of slowing down and digital media is certainly here to stay. Social sites such as Instagram will become market places for the various products. It is possible that Instagram will work as a link, matching people in need to the relevant retailer. It might go one step further and introduce direct selling from the site.

It is very likely that the top social media sites will merge with the less successful ones. There are only so many perspective customers on line and they will tire of checking several different streams only to be given the same information on each one. There is a distinct possibility that YouTube, Facebook and Instagram will be the dominant sites with the others fighting over what's left of the markets.

There is also the possibility that new social sites will be created and may affect the current status of any or even all the existing social media sites. Bad publicity can seriously damage any site and can happen at any time. Should this happen to any of the big players it is quite feasible that a new site would be created and do very well.

Instagram is well positioned to capitalise on the growing demand from the advertising market. There are already ads appearing on the site but the future will bring many more. Ads may well be built into posts and targeted by hashtag or users bios. There is the possibility of ads with one click sales technology to encourage spur of the moment sales. Advertisers are being forced to come up with new and innovative ways of marketing their products rather than the traditional banner ads. This means much more liaison between businesses and potential customers. Postings which directly advertise a product will be in competition with more subtle forms of advertising.

It is highly likely that the growth in followers over the last few years will continue at a similar pace. Instagram has become well known for being reliable and honest. It has a dedicated fan base which is expanding every year. The bigger its base becomes the more power it will have to influence marketing and other social trends. Big named companies will need to start negotiating with Instagram to ensure they are able to adequately represent themselves on the site and are not losing sales to newer, smaller and more nimble companies. Instagram is starting to make money from advertising and this trend will continue. They may well be other revenue streams appearing on Instagram as time passes in order to appease the parent company.

Technology is advancing at a frightening pace. People can now monitor everything going on around them and check information on the internet all from a watch on their wrist. Being so connected is good for social media sites like Instagram but will all this technology lead to a new way of linking with each other? It may not be a likely scenario in the immediate future but longer term virtual worlds may take over as the preferred way of connecting!

It is very likely that Instagram will become the place to spot new talent, styles or artists. As more and more people join the community the level of background chatter will increase which may make it difficult to spot the truly fresh or original content. It is very likely that Instagram will adapt and create new searches to allow for this.

In order to stay at the top of its game Instagram will need to change and adapt. This is something it has been very good at so far. In the future this change will be driven by its users and the market place. This will ensure it remains at the heart of the community for many years to come.

Links will probably be introduced, possibly for a charge. These will link back to the business website and allow someone to view entire catalogues and purchase accordingly. This has the potential to change the site as captions may no longer appear just a nice picture with an embedded link back to a site. This would not be making the most of the potential of Instagram but may be an effective marketing campaign for those new to the business.

What is certain is that Instagram is here to stay. Advertising executives will need to factor Instagram into their equations. Capital and resources will need to be invested into making the most of Instagram and regular monitoring of accounts will be essential to stay in touch with potential customers. It may be a place to share the highlights of what you have seen moment by moment but it is also a place where you can dare to dream. To shout from the rooftops of what you would like to be and to demonstrate in pictures just how good you are. Advertising executives may not be the only ones who can source information from this pond. Employment and talent scouts will be watching the site in case they come across the next best thing. Influential Instagramers will be targeted by companies to assist on promoting their products and local authorities will start using it to inform people of events or accidents in the area.

Instagram has the potential to be better than cell phones or text messages when communicating with a loved one. Not only is in instant but it is more expressive and provides a lasting memory. No site can ever become all things to all people but Instagram certainly has the potential to come close.

10666534R00023

Printed in Great Britain
by Amazon.co.uk, Ltd.,
Marston Gate.